DIARY OF A JESUS GIRL

PUBLISHERS

"Write all the words which I have spoken to you in a book." - Jeremiah 30:2

DIARY OF A JESUS GIRL Journal. Copyright © 2020. Crystal S. Daye.

All rights reserved. No part of this publication may be reproduced, distributed, or transmitted in any form or by any means, including photocopying, recording, or other electronic or mechanical methods, without the prior written permission of the publisher or author.

ISBN: 978-1-953759-25-2 (paperback)
ISBN: 978-1-953759-26-9 (hardback)

DAYELight
PUBLISHERS

Scriptures taken from the Holy Bible, New International Version®, NIV®. Copyright © 1973, 1978, 1984, 2011 by Biblica, Inc.™ Used by permission of Zondervan. All rights reserved worldwide. www.zondervan.com. The "NIV" and "New International Version" are trademarks registered in the United States Patent and Trademark Office by Biblica, Inc.™

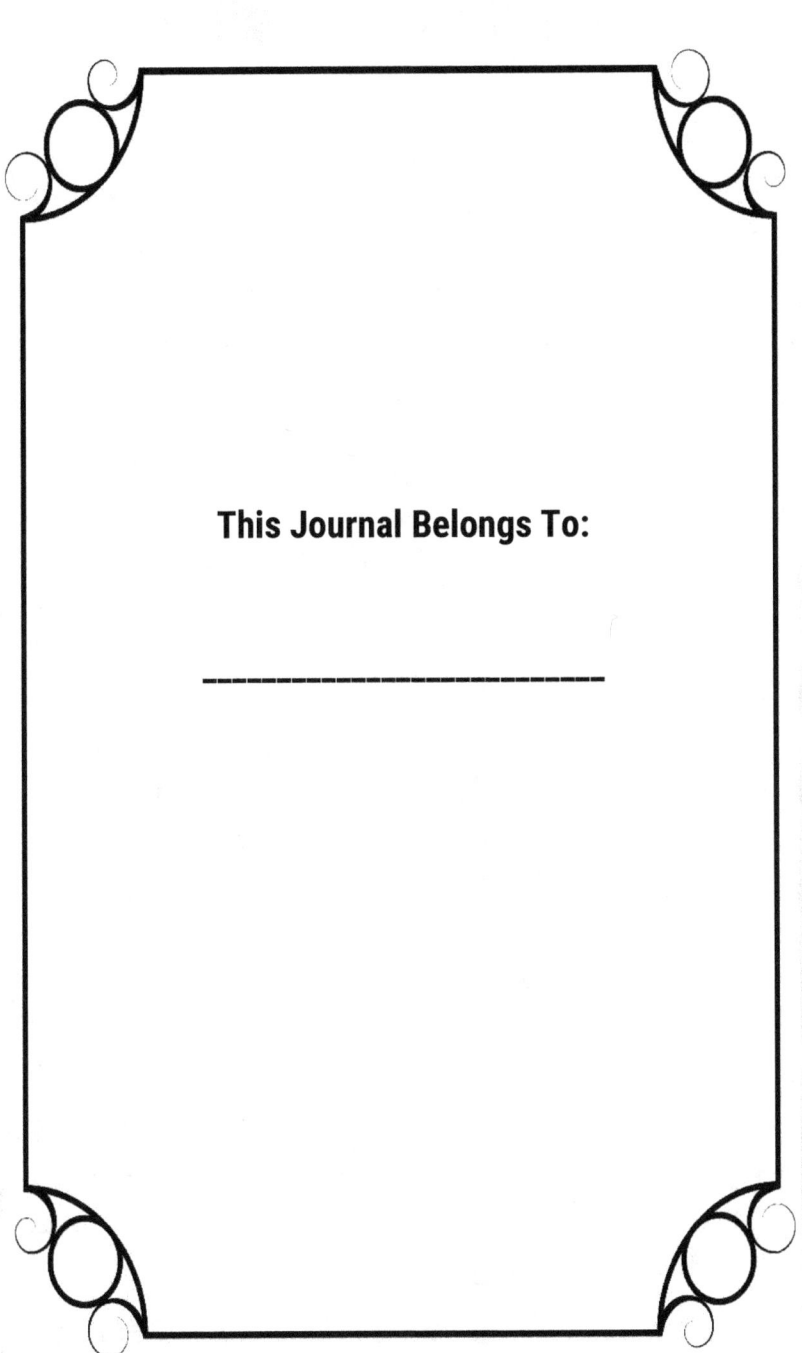

This Journal Belongs To:

_____

You are altogether beautiful, my darling; there is no flaw in you. (Sol. 4:7)

She is clothed with strength and dignity; she can laugh at the days to come. (Prov. 31:25)

You will be a crown of splendor in the LORD's hand, a royal diadem in the hand of your God. Is. 62:3

My beloved spoke and said to me, "Arise, my darling, my beautiful one, come with me. (Song 2:10)

She opens her mouth with wisdom, and the teaching of kindness is on her tongue. (Prov. 31:26)

Those who look to him are radiant, and their faces shall never be ashamed. (Ps. 34:5)

Your workmanship is marvelous – how well I know it. (Psalm 139:13 – 14)

For we are God's masterpiece... (Eph. 2:10)

...Created to do good works which God prepared in advance for us to do. (Eph. 2:10)

Blessed is she who has believed that the Lord would fulfill his promises to her! (Lu. 1:45)

God is within her, she will not fall; God will help her at break of day.
(Ps. 46:5)

And who knows but that you have come to your royal position for such a time as this? (Es. 4:14)

But you are a chosen generation, a royal priesthood, a holy nation, His own special people.... (1 Peter 2:9)

For our citizenship is in heaven, from which we also eagerly wait for the Savior, the Lord Jesus Christ. (Phil. 3:20)

Blessed are the pure in heart, for they shall see God. (Mt. 5:8)

Now you are the body of Christ and individually members of it. (1 Cor. 12:27)

You are not your own, for you were bought with a price. (1 Cor. 6:20)

See, I have inscribed you on the palms of My hands... (Is. 49:16)

I have been crucified with Christ; it is no longer I who live, but Christ lives in me.... (Gal. 2:20)

And, "I will be a Father to you, and you will be my sons and daughters, says the Lord Almighty." (2 Cor. 6:18)

For in Christ Jesus you are all sons (and daughters) of God, through faith. (Gal. 3:26)

...the glorious riches of this mystery, which is Christ in you, the hope of glory. (Col. 1:27)

I have called you friends, for all that I have heard from my Father I have made known to you. (Jo. 15:15)

Therefore, my dear brothers and sisters, stand firm. Let nothing move you. (1 Cor. 15:58)

But to all who did receive him, who believed in his name, he gave the right to become children of God. (Jo. 1:12)

For you have died, and your life is hidden with Christ in God. (Col. 3:3)

And to put on the new self, created after the likeness of God in true righteousness and holiness. (Eph. 4:24)

So God created mankind in his own image... (Gen. 1:27)

Delight yourself in the Lord and He will give you the desires of your heart – Psalm 37:4

The Lord Himself goes before you and will be with you: He will never leave you nor forsake you – Deuteronomy 31:8

I can do all things through Christ, who gives me strength – Philippians 4:13

This is the confidence which we have before Him, that, if we ask anything according to His will, He hears us. - 1 John 5:14

And my God will supply all your needs according to His riches in glory in Christ Jesus. - Philippians 4:19

But if any of you lacks wisdom, let him ask of God, who gives to all generously and without reproach, and it will be given to him. - James 1:5

that the God of our Lord Jesus Christ, the Father of glory, may give to you a spirit of wisdom and of revelation in the knowledge of Him.
- Ephesians 1:17

in everything give thanks; for this is God's will for you in Christ Jesus. - 1 Thessalonians 5:18

always giving thanks for all things in the name of our Lord Jesus Christ to God, even the Father; - Ephesians 5:20

Thanks be to God for His indescribable gift! - 2 Corinthians 9:15

Be anxious for nothing, but in everything by prayer and supplication with thanksgiving let your requests be made known to God. Philippians 4:6

"For God has not given us a spirit of fear and timidity, but of power, love, and self-discipline." - 2 Timothy 1:7

"'For I know the plans I have for you,' says the Lord. 'They are plans for good and not for disaster, to give you a future and a hope.' - Jeremiah 29:11

"The Lord himself will fight for you. Just stay calm." - Exodus 14:14

"Rejoice in our confident hope. Be patient in trouble, and keep on praying." - Romans 12:12

"Let us hold tightly without wavering to the hope we affirm, for God can be trusted to keep his promise" - Hebrews 10:23

"Search for the Lord and for his strength; continually seek him." - 1 Chronicles 16:11

"If you look for me wholeheartedly, you will find me." - Jeremiah 29:13

You are altogether beautiful, my darling; there is no flaw in you.
(Sol. 4:7)

She is clothed with strength and dignity; she can laugh at the days to come. (Prov. 31:25)

You will be a crown of splendor in the LORD's hand, a royal diadem in the hand of your God. Is. 62:3

My beloved spoke and said to me, "Arise, my darling, my beautiful one, come with me. (Song 2:10)

She opens her mouth with wisdom, and the teaching of kindness is on her tongue. (Prov. 31:26)

Those who look to him are radiant, and their faces shall never be ashamed. (Ps. 34:5)

Your workmanship is marvelous – how well I know it. (Psalm 139:13 – 14)

For we are God's masterpiece... (Eph. 2:10)

...Created to do good works which God prepared in advance for us to do. (Eph. 2:10)

Blessed is she who has believed that the Lord would fulfill his promises to her! (Lu. 1:45)

God is within her, she will not fall; God will help her at break of day. (Ps. 46:5)

And who knows but that you have come to your royal position for such a time as this? (Es. 4:14)

But you are a chosen generation, a royal priesthood, a holy nation, His own special people…. (1 Peter 2:9)

For our citizenship is in heaven, from which we also eagerly wait for the Savior, the Lord Jesus Christ. (Phil. 3:20)

Blessed are the pure in heart, for they shall see God. (Mt. 5:8)

Now you are the body of Christ and individually members of it. (1 Cor. 12:27)

You are not your own, for you were bought with a price. (1 Cor. 6:20)

See, I have inscribed you on the palms of My hands... (Is. 49:16)

I have been crucified with Christ; it is no longer I who live, but Christ lives in me…. (Gal. 2:20)

And, "I will be a Father to you, and you will be my sons and daughters, says the Lord Almighty." (2 Cor. 6:18)

For in Christ Jesus you are all sons (and daughters) of God, through faith. (Gal. 3:26)

..the glorious riches of this mystery, which is Christ in you, the hope of glory. (Col. 1:27)

I have called you friends, for all that I have heard from my Father I have made known to you. (Jo. 15:15)

Therefore, my dear brothers and sisters, stand firm. Let nothing move you. (1 Cor. 15:58)

But to all who did receive him, who believed in his name, he gave the right to become children of God. (Jo. 1:12)

For you have died, and your life is hidden with Christ in God. (Col. 3:3)

And to put on the new self, created after the likeness of God in true righteousness and holiness. (Eph. 4:24)

So God created mankind in his own image... (Gen. 1:27)

Delight yourself in the Lord and He will give you the desires of your heart – Psalm 37:4

The Lord Himself goes before you and will be with you: He will never leave you nor forsake you – Deuteronomy 31:8

I can do all things through Christ, who gives me strength – Philippians 4:13

This is the confidence which we have before Him, that, if we ask anything according to His will, He hears us. - 1 John 5:14

And my God will supply all your needs according to His riches in glory in Christ Jesus. - Philippians 4:19

But if any of you lacks wisdom, let him ask of God, who gives to all generously and without reproach, and it will be given to him. - James 1:5

that the God of our Lord Jesus Christ, the Father of glory, may give to you a spirit of wisdom and of revelation in the knowledge of Him.
- Ephesians 1:17

in everything give thanks; for this is God's will for you in Christ Jesus. - 1 Thessalonians 5:18

always giving thanks for all things in the name of our Lord Jesus Christ to God, even the Father; - Ephesians 5:20

Thanks be to God for His indescribable gift! - 2 Corinthians 9:15

Be anxious for nothing, but in everything by prayer and supplication with thanksgiving let your requests be made known to God. Philippians 4:6

"For God has not given us a spirit of fear and timidity, but of power, love, and self-discipline." - 2 Timothy 1:7

"'For I know the plans I have for you,' says the Lord. 'They are plans for good and not for disaster, to give you a future and a hope.' - Jeremiah 29:11

www.ingramcontent.com/pod-product-compliance
Lightning Source LLC
Chambersburg PA
CBHW071447070526
44578CB00001B/239